High Tide, Low Tide

Mick Manning
and Brita Granström

Shags and cormorants
stretch their wings out to
dry after a swim.

W
FRANKLIN WATTS

For Muriel Manning

First published in 2001
by Franklin Watts,
96 Leonard Street,
London EC2A 4XD

Franklin Watts Australia
56 O'Riordan Street
Alexandria
NSW 2015

The illustrations in this book have been drawn
by both Mick and Brita

Text and illustrations © 2001 Mick Manning
and Brita Granström
Series editor: Rachel Cooke
Art director: Jonathan Hair

Printed in Hong Kong, China
A CIP catalogue record is available from
the British Library.
Dewey Classification 551.47
ISBN 0 7496 4181 9

Contents

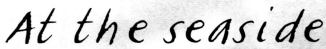

At the seaside

. . . and sand in our sandwiches!

The tide comes in and goes out twice every day. It takes about 12 ¹/₂ hours between each high tide, so the times of high tide and low tide change each day.

7

. . . and waving at fishing boats chugging out on the ebbing tide . . .

. . . and licking ice-creams!

Boats leave harbour just after high tide. The turning tide 'pulls out', taking the boats with it.

9

Low tide

hermit crab

spiny squat lobster

Lugworms tunnel
under the sand. They
push up worm-shaped
'casts' as they go.

crab →

At low tide, you can spot all sorts of tracks. Prints left by people, seabirds and crabs criss-cross the sand.

beetle

fox

wader

gull

Lots of animals search the beach for food. Some dig for worms, others scavenge for scraps washed up by the waves.

13

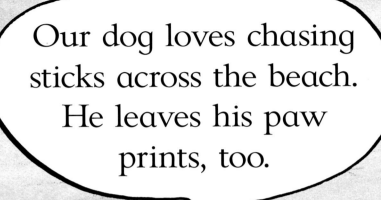

Our dog loves chasing sticks across the beach. He leaves his paw prints, too.

Ripple marks are left as the waves move out with the tide.

And dog dirt! YUCK!

Dog dirt spreads dangerous germs so clear up after your dog.

15

The tide turns

Wading birds follow the tide, feeding at the water's edge.

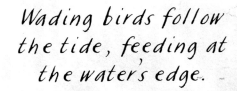

But the tide always comes back in again. The waves lap up the beach, cleaning as they come.

Oil spills from ships poison the sea.

The oil injures and kills seabirds and waders too.

merganser

grey plover

golden plover

shag

lapwing

dunlin

godwit

sanderling

redshank

curlew

ringed plover

oystercatcher

17

High tide

At high tide, we gaze down from the cliff tops. It seems like the beach has disappeared!

DANGER!
Never go close to the
edge of a cliff. It is easy
to slip and fall.

Wild grasses
hold sand-dunes
together and
stop the sand
blowing away.

21

The tide turns again!
I close my eyes and listen
to the waves roll in and suck
back across the shingle . . .

. . . leaving wet, smooth pebbles, perfect for skimming stones!

Pebbles are worn smooth from years of tumbling in the waves and sand.

23

Beachcombers

At low tide, we love to go beachcombing.

You never know what the tide will wash up – shells, driftwood, rubbish from a passing ship or even something from a country far away across the sea.

26

Explore the seaside

Become a tide-watcher next time you go to the seaside.

Time the tides
Record the times of high tide and low tide each day. Check your record against a tide chart.

weever fish

Beachcombing
Beachcombing is part of the fun of the seaside. You can collect shells and pebbles or things washed up by the tide. Don't disturb animals or pick wild flowers, though. Draw them instead and try to find out their names.

flotsam and jetsam

Safety by the sea

Be careful at the seaside:

• Don't climb cliffs or play close to their edge.

• Make sure you don't go to places where you can be cut off by the tide.

• Wear shoes or wellies to protect your feet from stinging weever and jelly fish.

• Don't pick up sharp or rusty things, needles or syringes.

Map-maker

Make a map of your favourite place by the sea. Show all the things that are special to you – from rockpools to ice-cream vans.

my seaside map:

nesting birds

sea

caravan

dunes

lighthouse

pier

ice-cream van

sandbar

sandy beach

breakwater

pebble beach

rockpools

harbour

Tide words and index

beach A stretch of sand or shingle which slopes gently into the sea. Pages 6, 14, 16, 20, 24

ebbing Going down or flowing out. Page 9

high tide The highest point of the tide. Pages 6, 7, 9, 18, 26

low tide The lowest point of the tide. Pages 6, 7, 10, 11, 13, 24, 26

oil spills Oil is the black, sticky liquid used to make petrol. It is transported in huge ships. If there is an accident, the oil spills out and floats on the water. Page 16

rockpools Pools of sea-water formed as the tide goes out. They disappear again when it comes in. Page 11

sand-dunes Huge piles of sand built up by the wind and sea. Pages 20, 21

scavenge To feed off rubbish or dead animals which have been killed by something else. Page 13

shingle Lots of pebbles piled together. Page 22

tide The movement of the sea in and out across the land. Tides are caused by an invisible pull on the water by the Moon as it moves around the Earth. The invisible pull is called gravity. Pages 7, 9, 11, 14, 16, 22, 24

waves The rounded ridges of water that build up on the sea as a result of the wind and the movement of the tides. Pages 6, 13, 14, 16, 22, 23